Unscramble Your Life

How to find direction and success in the chaos of adult life

Nick Salmon

For my children - who teach me more every day than any book could!

And my darling wife - who told me to do this!

Contents

Modern Life 7

Get Out of Bed 14

Affirmations 23

Four Quadrants 33

Self 41

Health 50

Wealth 60

Future 72

Take Action 82

Your First Week 92

Over To You...104

About Nick Salmon 105

Modern Life

I want to start by telling you a story.

Imagine you're a young person. You got a good level of education and found yourself a reasonably good job. You were lucky enough that one night in a bar you met your future partner and after a few years of dating one of you finally pops the question and you get married.

Shortly after being married you scrape together just enough money between you for a deposit for a house. Nothing fancy but it was your first home. You live together in blissful harmony without a care in the world. You travel. You shop. You go out to bars and restaurants. You party and laugh with friends. You work hard but play hard too.

Then one day you decide to have children. After "trying" your best you are blessed with your beautiful first-born child. Your world stops revolving for the first few days as you fall deeply in love with this new little person you have created together.

And then life really gets going…

Fast-forward five years; you perhaps have two children by now, a constant childcare merry-go-round, mounting debts, mountains of laundry and a lifestyle that feels full of obligations and chores.

No matter how hard you try you still can't get on top of things. You're both now working absolutely flat-out. You never feel relaxed or well rested. Social engagements seem to have turned into an elaborate logistics operation, where no one seems able to enjoy themselves or even finish a sentence without a distraction. You've become the people you never thought you would be!

There is never enough time to look forward and plan things ahead. You are permanently in reactive or "firefighting" mode. There's always another bill to pay, something to fix, a call to return or a child screaming.

Your career seems to be floundering. You had some initial success and everybody thought you'll *go far* but now things seem to have gone a bit stale. After some early promotions, that next step has either lost its shine or is slipping further out of your grasp.

There never seems to be enough time to just be. You long to just sit quietly or truly enjoy quality time as a family.

Your life is totally scrambled!

A Typical Day

In the mornings you wake up tired and exhausted. You're just about able to roll over and grab your phone to shut off the alarm. Then you see the work emails.

Hundreds and hundreds of emails, that seem to have flooded in from this mystical place overnight. Somebody in accounts who needs a report so urgently they have to email you at 11 PM. A project you've been working on for three months has unraveled overnight. Or there's a capital investment decision that needs to be made by lunchtime or the world will end. You need to tackle all this within 30 seconds of waking up!

Carrying that weight on your shoulders, you slump into the shower and you think of nothing else but work, the bills you haven't paid, what's for dinner or is one of your kids sick? You're mentally and physically exhausted before you even start the day.

Then the children wake up and need feeding and dressing; but at their own pace. Every day they seem to move at a slower speed – trying their upmost to make you late for work. There's always a row about something - what clothes to wear or what's for breakfast. Finally you strap them in a car seat and drive like a maniac to a childcare facility that you're not really sure about. Every other place has a waiting list and you need a solution now – so this is it!

You stumble through the workday, constantly battling with others to achieve the simplest of tasks that have somehow become impossible with modern bureaucracy. We're told that our employer cares about our "well-being" but benefits and perks seem to be evaporating on a daily basis. You don't want to sit on a beanbag or hot-desk next to a load of other people yelling loudly into their cell phones. You don't know where you see yourself in five years time but it's definitely not with this company.

You battle the clock all day before leaving late and tearing home – hoping that someone remembered to get the kids. Dinner every evening is just a mission to get something edible on the table. Then there's a mad sprint to get the children into bed so you and your spouse can have some alone time. You spend this time either on your phones or laptops working or watching Netflix in different rooms.

Finally, utterly shattered, you crawl into bed.

Sound familiar? You are not alone. This is the typical lifestyle of an adult today. A hybrid of the cynicism of Generation X and the electronic addictions of Millennials.

This was my life, but then I picked up a book.

The Trip

One October day I took a business trip. I travel quite regularly with my iPod (yes I still have one!) and my work laptop. For some strange reason, before I left the house, I asked my wife if she had a book I could read. Don't misunderstand me; I've taken many trips with many books that I never read. She gave me the Miracle Morning by Hal Elrod and I stuffed it into my bag without a second look.

After an hour or so on the plane I stopped looking at emails and went to fire up my trusty iPod. But nothing happened. Disaster. What was I going to do now? After gazing out the window and trying desperately to sleep, I took the time to do something I haven't done in 10 years. I reached into my bag and pulled out a book and started to read.

The book was excellent and one that I'll talk about more later; but on that Boeing 737 at 35,000 feet that morning I couldn't stop thinking about one question:

Is this really the way I want to be living?

Hundreds of personal development books will try and sell on the radical improvements they are going to make to your life – you'll be a millionaire, you'll have a six pack, you'll be adored by others. My message is subtler.

Unscramble Your Life

By adopting the simple Four Quadrant principle I explain in this book; you will unscramble your life and get out of the chaos!

It's that simple.

I've got out of the chaos. I no longer feel exhausted or buried. I get up earlier and I'm more productive. I have quality time with my wife and kids. I've kept the same job but rediscovered my career. I've kept the same house but now have time to keep it clean and tidy. My bank balance is creeping up and I have more money saving ideas and investments still to implement. I've even written this book in my free time!

In the next few pages, I will explain my Four Quadrant approach to rediscovering your direction and starting to achieve your goals.

I have found this framework infinitely powerful in getting my life back on track; increasing my happiness and helping me reconnect with my family.

I want to share these tools with you in this book so you too can achieve the same levels of happiness and success.

For those of you reading who don't have a family or a partner at this point in your life, you're going to get fed up with some of the references to spouse or children but the power of the Four Quadrant model can be applied to anyone's life.

Guess what, I kept on reading too. In the six weeks following the epiphany I had on the plane, I read a total of ten self-improvement books. Almost the entire bestsellers list including The 4-Hour Workweek, Rich Dad Poor Dad, The Wealthy Barber, The Seven Habits of Highly Effective People, The Secret and many others. You'll find them referenced throughout my book including a summary of their key themes. Now you can just read one book and get the benefits of many - saving you time and money!

You can also visit my website (**www.unscrambleyourlife.com**) and read my latest book reviews for free as well as my blog and other great sources of inspiration and information.

I'm ready to help you unscramble your life so let's get started.

Get Out of Bed

The first step to reestablishing a grip on your life is very easy.

Get out of bed.

Before you groan and throw this book out, I want to get something clear – I was not a "morning person" but I have become one by following a very simple process.

We have all heard the phrases "the early bird catches the worm" or "first come, first served" so we already know that getting up early is a smart thing to do.

I'm sure many of us would start our perfect day watching the sunrise while sipping coffee and flicking through a good book. A true sense of calm and paradise. We all want to experience paradise every day right? We should all leap out of bed to enjoy this little slice of heaven before we get on with our day.

But we don't, we roll over when the alarm goes off and hit the snooze button. We didn't get enough sleep. Now our phone has started buzzing and here come the emails. There's stuff we didn't get done yesterday, more stuff to do today and things we can't possibly think about for tomorrow.

The complete book on getting up early was written by Hal Elrod. I strongly advise anybody undertaking my Four Quadrant method to read this book if they are serious about improving their life.

Elrod gives you some fantastic advice on how to get out of bed early. I follow his powerful S.A.V.E.R.S. mantra every morning and start everyday with a smile on my face and feeling energized!

The Miracle Morning – Hal Elrod

This is the definitive book on how to define a life changing morning routine! Elrod explains his Life S.A.V.E.R.S. mantra for having a successful morning. This stands for:
Silence – first take time to meditate and relax
Affirmations – focus on your goals
Visualizations – visualize your goals
Exercise – get your blood pumping
Reading – educate yourself
Scribing – take notes or journal
I can't do the content justice in this brief synopsis but this book has truly changed my life and has some essential principles that will help you maximize your use of the concepts I present in my book.

You too can become one of those irritating "morning people" who are wide-awake no matter how early it is! I truly believe anyone can do this and it doesn't involve any drugs – not even coffee!

While I freely admit Elrod is the guru on this topic, here are some tools and techniques I've found essential to get me out of bed in the morning.

Tell Yourself You're Going To Get Enough Sleep

There are lots of articles and books that have been published on the importance of getting the right amount of sleep. However there is no universal agreement on what the "right" amount actually is. In fact how much sleep you, as an individual need is a question only you can answer.

As a parent of young children, the amount of sleep I get varies wildly! I also travel quite often which messes up my body clock. While I always function at my best when I've had 7-8 hours sleep, life won't always allow me that luxury.

One of the best techniques I found to mange this is from Elrod. Just before I go to sleep, I look at the clock and work out how much sleep I'm likely to get. Say its 5 hours. I then make sure that one of the last thoughts I have before I fall asleep is

"Five hours is plenty of sleep and I'm going to feel refreshed in the morning."

Just that one sentence has transformed how rested I feel in the morning. The lowest number I've tried is 3 hours and while I won't say it wasn't a struggle the next morning, I did still feel energized to start my day.

This process has also had a weird side effect. After a few weeks of trying it, I started waking up naturally a few minutes before my alarm! It's been an amazing turnaround for a guy who used to hit snooze at least 3 times before even stirring!

Try it tonight and see how you feel in the morning.

Hide Your Phone

Hide your phone, tablet, laptop or any other device that can get email, texts or any kind of status updates. If it's your alarm clock, buy a cheap one from Amazon. Spending your last waking minutes of the day starring at endless streams of information will set your mind racing at a time when you're trying to unwind and relax. Equally having something buzzing or flashing by your bed throughout the night is going to have an effect on how well you sleep.

The other bonus of not having your phone within arms reach is it removes the temptation to check it as soon as you wake up. This will again divert your mind from your primary objective - getting up and starting your day.

If you are too cheap to buy a separate alarm clock, at a minimum place your device on the other side of the room. This will at least get you out of bed and moving before you pick it up. But don't even think of opening any apps and turn off your alerts so nothing catches your eye! You need to be protective of your thoughts first thing in the morning, as they will have a profound affect on your day.

This leads nicely into my next tip.

Banish Negativity

Make sure you surround yourself with positive thoughts in the morning. It's a great time to reflect and be grateful.

Taking a couple of moments to think about what went well yesterday and what you are grateful for today will help spring you out of bed.

I try and complete one small, positive task first thing in the morning. The night before, I write down what it will be on a piece of paper next to my alarm clock. That way it's the first thing I see when I wake up.

They're normally really easy things like making my wife a coffee or writing a text to someone who helped or supported me the day before. I've even found the small act of paying a bill can make me feel a sense of accomplishment having only been awake for a few minutes!

These small "micro goals" can set up your whole day with a positive feeling. We've all heard someone ask if you "got out of the wrong side of the bed". This statement is actually all about the attitude that you've started your day with and these positive, grateful tasks are a great way to get you on the right path.

Conversely, avoid starting the day with a negative act, like watching the news. Many of us fall into this trap because we want to be informed about current affairs.

While I agree it's important to be aware of what's going on in the world around you, so much of the media focus on negative acts – crime, war, political arguments and even bad weather. Introducing this negativity in the early hours can spoil the rest of your day.

Avoid other potentially negative things like checking your bank balance or getting the mail and finding more bills to pay! Again, like the news, these are important daily activities but leave them for your lunch break - by which time you will have already conquered the day!

Use Light

Human beings need light. So much so that we've invented a medical term for when we don't get enough of it – Seasonal Affective Disorder or SAD for short. It's a mild form of depression that people can experience during the winter months due to a lack of sunlight.

Obviously the inverse of this – lots of sunlight – makes us happy and energetic and that's exactly how we need to feel in the morning.

Stumbling around in the dark looking for a pair of clean socks can make us grumpy and miserable; and that's before we stub our toe on the foot of the bed!

But if we fling open the curtains or turn on the lights we instantly feel more awake. So get a little light into your life as soon as you wake up.

While this may be too brutal a start for some, special alarms clocks exist that gradually increase the light in the room until you "naturally" wake up. I have used one of these in the winter months and it makes a massive difference to how I feel in the morning.

This method may not be too popular if you share your bedroom with someone but why not sneak into the bathroom, kitchen or living room and start "shedding some light on the matter" as soon as you get up.

No Excuses

Getting up early is a solo sport. It is 100% within your control. No one else can make you get up but more importantly no one can stop you!

There really are no excuses. I have done my morning routine on an airplane, in different time zones, in hotel rooms, on my front porch and even with a hangover (it's actually a great cure!).

We get very good at justifying the things we don't achieve as someone else's fault. Here are some great excuses for not getting up in the morning – a car alarm went off, my kids were up in the night, the dog was barking.

All are real life events that can happen to any of us but the difference is how you respond to them. How ridiculous is it to blame your lack of motivation or success on a dog? Don't let anything get in your way!

By now you've understood the importance of reading the Miracle Morning (or at least watching a You Tube review of it) and getting yourself out of bed earlier. I can't stress this enough. If you truly want to reclaim control of your life and start driving it in the direction you want; you need to start every day off right. Get up and get into a routine of reflection, positive thinking, exercise and personal development.

It may sound trivial, but an extra 30 - 60 minutes of focused positive time and exercise can drastically improve your mindset, increase your productivity and help you establish direction and purpose. I know this from personal experience and from others that I've talked with who have equally positive and structured morning routines.

Not sure where to begin, don't worry. In the chapter called Your First Week, I'll help you get "up and at 'em" in just seven days! In the meantime, why not try one of the suggestions in this chapter tomorrow morning and start getting yourself back on top.

Affirmations

An affirmation is an assertion or statement that something is true. They are widely used to help train our brain to embrace something new.

I have always thought affirmations were nonsense! How can saying something over and over again make it become real? Equally the whole concept of standing and staring at myself in the mirror while I recited that nonsense felt ridiculous.

I would be embarrassed to tell my friends. It's the kind of thing you do in secret and never tell anyone about.

But once I started, the reality for me has been very different. Just by saying words doesn't make something come true but it does keep it fresh in your mind. I'll give you an example.

When I began my journey of self-improvement, one of my first affirmations was:

I will lose 10lbs by Christmas.

I said that every morning for six weeks leading up to Christmas. Did saying those words alone make me lose 10 lbs. of fat in just six weeks? No, they didn't, but they did do one thing; they kept it current in my mind.

Standing up every morning and reciting that statement meant that my brain absorbed it into my sub-conscious.

What that means, in practice, is the next time I'm standing in line to buy a coffee in front of all the delicious muffins or somebody's very kindly home baked some cookies and brought them into the office; rather picking one up and shoving it in my mouth without thinking... I pause.

This pause is my inner voice telling me "you're never going to lose 10 lbs. by Christmas if you shove that triple chocolate donut in your face". That for me is the true power of affirmations. Affirmations are the cornerstone of the Four Quadrant method and embracing them is essential to your success.

They aren't easy to pick up and you'll need to iterate. You will have doubts and there will be naysayers. In the next few pages, I'm going to give you some hints and tips on how to get affirmations to work for you.

Visualize Instead

As I described, I struggled with affirmations, but visualizations were a lot easier.

Close your eyes and picture yourself doing something you've always wanted to do.

Maybe it's exhilarating like skydiving or driving a sports car or it could be less extreme like acing an important meeting with a client or a senior manager.

Picture yourself in that situation. Walk through it step-by-step in your head from the moment you board the plane, start the car or walk into the conference room. You feel excited, powerful and confident; these great emotions surge through you and you feel like a winner.

Now take that image and turn it into a sentence:

I will skydive
I will drive a Mustang
I will ace the meeting

Now every time you say that affirmation, unlock that visualization in your mind and feel the energy flow.

Be Positive

The key to making the Four Quadrant tool successful is to have strong affirmations that you truly believe in.

One of the primary struggles that I had with affirmations in the beginning was that I just didn't believe in them. I was saying all the right things, but deep down I honestly did not feel I was ever going to achieve them.

This negative foundation meant that I was never going to succeed. You need a positive attitude to be open to affirmations. If you struggle with this – and most of us do – try this little exercise.

Get up one morning, look at yourself in the mirror and recite the following:

I will be a positive person today

Feels really awkward doesn't it? Maybe say it a couple of times and try to make your voice sound genuine! Then, throughout the day, try reminding yourself of the commitment you made in the morning. When you're starting to moan about how bad the traffic is or how irritating a person on TV is - stop. Bring yourself back to the affirmation and recite it.

How much better do you feel as you go about your day? Do you get any surprisingly positive outcomes?

I'm still in the early days of trying out this strategy but it has made me feel better about myself and I can sense more positive opportunities coming my way.

This is how I started; just trying to be more positive about situations that arise during the day. There is an interesting book that discusses the power of thinking and positive thought called The Secret.

The Secret – Rhonda Byrne

Byrne suggests that just by thinking about things, you can make them appear in your life. The main theme is a three-step process: ask, believe and receive. She also underlines the importance of gratitude and visualization in achieving your goals. The Universe wants you to be successful, you just have to open your mind to it!

When I first encountered the concepts in this book I was pretty skeptical, but I have come to respect the high level principle that positive thoughts do get positive outcomes. The concepts in this book are also in a film of the same name, which is available on Netflix, so why not watch it tonight!

I am not a religious person myself but I have observed that a lot of people who do have strong faith also have a positive outlook on life. I believe this positivity is linked to prayer.

By praising and honoring a divine being, on a regular basis, they are in fact making a series of positive affirmations. For example:

God is great. God loves me.

These statements give us a warmness and positive feeling that we can carry into our daily lives. Why not go to your local church for a few weeks and see how if this helps you adopt a positive outlook.

I strongly encourage you to try a few positive thinking experiments and see how your outlook and energy change. It should become much easier to write affirmations after that.

Repetition

Repetition is key to embedding ideas in our brain. As children we are taught the alphabet and numbers through continuous repetition of sequences:

A,B,C,D,E....1,2,3,4,5,6,7,8,9,10.

These repetitions help to train our brain to store valuable information.

Affirmations are the same. In order to store them in our minds, we need to repeat them regularly. If you find it helps, say each affirmation five times in a row. For me personally, once a day is enough but do some experiments and see what sticks.

I also prefer once a day as it allows me to focus my energy on ensuring that I am sincere with every statement. I find constantly repeating something 67 times means it loses its impact on me and I just go through the motions. Again find a rhythm that works for you.

Want Them To Be True

Another reason I found that affirmations don't work is that we don't really want them to become true. For example:

I will quit my day job and go and live on the beach.

This sounds fantastic! We'd all love to live on a desert island and not have to go to work, wouldn't we? However, internally the reality is terrifying us! Leaving the security of a stable job with company benefits just sounds crazy and there aren't many "good schools" on desert islands.

You have to know what you want and know why you want it. We'll cover the "why" bit in more detail later on. For now, just remember that any affirmation you make you have to understand the "why" behind it. This will make sure that deep down you want them to be true.

Use The Right Words

Affirmations tend to be "I will" statements and this language sometimes doesn't work for a lot of us. It makes us feel awkward or uneasy.

Equally if you're staring at a page of just "I will" statements there is a risk that the importance of each one is lost as the language blurs together. So try and vary the words you use in your affirmations. Try "I am going to" or "I shall".

Similarly sometimes affirmations are not our own ideas. We've taken them from somebody else; a book we read, a poster we saw, a celebrity blog or a T-shirt in Walmart.

While all these areas can be great sources of inspiration, your affirmations have to be exactly that – yours! Again try and tweak the statements you find to match your way of speaking otherwise they just won't fit quite right.

I prefer to use "I will" type statements as I'm most comfortable with that language; but I've also tried some present tense language like "I am" or "I enjoy". For example:

I enjoy daily exercise

This language helps you feel that your affirmations are close and achievable today rather than something that may be further in the future.

They Don't Have To Be Perfect

Don't try and overachieve with your affirmations. This sounds counterintuitive as affirmations are meant to push us to succeed but they need to be digestible.

Having an affirmation that is more than one sentence is either too large for your brain to manage or too detailed and prescriptive for your creative juices to get excited about. You don't need to reach perfection with your first attempt. The most important thing is to get something down on paper.

Your affirmations are dynamic, flexible and moldable and so you can shape them as you go along. You may be familiar with the Pareto Principle or the "80:20" rule. The idea is that 80% of your results come from 20% of your actions. Focus here on getting the right ideas down initially (the 20% part) and start using them to get results (the 80% part)!

The detail and accuracy of them can evolve over time as you learn and grow. Trust me you are going to get to know your affirmations very well and so you'll always be finding new ways to improve them.

This chapter is just a quick drive-by of some of the pitfalls I encountered with my affirmations. There's plenty of material online and in other books on how to define and grow your affirmations but you've now got some basics to get started.

In the next chapter I'll tell you how to organize your affirmations in my Four Quadrant tool and really start making them work for you.

Four Quadrants

So far, I've explained some of the basics you need to master in order to unscramble your life. You know that you need to get up in the morning and you are starting to understand affirmations and how they can work for you.

Now it's time to put some structure in place that will help you generate and categorize your affirmations.

Your Life Needs A Plan

I want to start with a question.

How many projects or big tasks do you do, either at work or at home, without a plan?

Imagine that your company is acquiring a new $5 million piece of machinery. Would you walk into your boss's office and say:

We need $5 million for a new machine that we're going to buy soon and will pay for itself at some point. Can I have approval please?

Is he going to reach in the drawer and pull out his checkbook? No. More likely he's going to have lots of questions for you:

When will the machine arrive?
How long will it take to get up and running?
Who will maintain it?
When will I get my money back?

He wants to understand your long-term strategy and know that you have a detailed plan to succeed.

Let's take another example from our home life.

You have decided you want to buy a house. One of the first steps you take is to talk to your bank or a mortgage lender to understand what you can afford. You'll then hire a realtor who can help develop your criteria and start guiding you through the process.

In this case, your realtor brings the plan and structure you need to succeed in your house purchase.

Try and think of a task that you do where you don't have a clear plan? Even with things like grocery shopping most people take a list so they don't forget something. Their list is their plan for success!

Plans help us achieve our goals in a structured efficient way, yet how many of us have a plan for how we want to live our life? I'm guessing the answer is not many. Indeed, I didn't until a couple of years ago. Hence I was just drifting from one task to the next without really understanding where I was going or what I wanted.

In today's chaotic lifestyle, we all tend to focus on the area of our lives that is causing the most immediate issues and prioritize those tasks! My TV broke so I need to research and buy another one today. This behavior means we neglect other, less urgent areas, like our retirement planning or our health; but these are far more important than buying a TV.

It fascinates me that for the biggest project we ever have to complete; our life, very few of us have any kind of long-term plan or strategy. We can all think of examples where poor project planning has led to cost and schedule overruns or an unsatisfactory result at the end. Without a life plan, we spend more money than we have and we either achieve our goals too late in life to enjoy them or we never achieve them at all!

But starting from today, using the Four Quadrant method, you will have a life plan. If you follow it, manage it and develop it, you are guaranteed to unscramble your life and achieve your goals. That's exactly what I did and it can all fit on one piece of paper!

One Piece Of Paper

When I talked about plans for a project or task at work, I'm sure some of you thought of elaborate Gantt charts with hundreds of milestones. Surely your life plan, with all its infinite complexities needs pages of detail?

Wrong. We need to take our life plan with us everywhere we go so it needs to be simple enough for us to memorize. I developed the Four Quadrant method to help make my life plan exactly that, simple and memorable.

Now you're going to make your Four Quadrant template in five easy steps:

1. *Grab a piece of paper. Plain or lined – doesn't matter.*

2. *Fold it in half and then in half again.*

3. *Open it out. You should be looking at four equal sized squares or rectangles – these are your Four Quadrants.*

4. *Across the very top of page, write "Today is going to be great because..."*

5. *In the bottom left block, write the heading "Self". In the block to the right of it put "Health". In the top left block (under "Today is going to be great because...") write "Wealth" and in the final block to the right, put "Future"*

Great, your Four Quadrant template is complete! It should look something like the picture below.

So what do all these headings mean? Here's a quick summary of the areas of your life they are focused on:

SELF - This is where you capture and understand your personal beliefs and motivations.

HEALTH - This Quadrant is where you'll address health, exercise and wellbeing goals.

WEALTH - This section covers how you will manage your finances and plans to grow your wealth.

FUTURE - This final part is where you capture your personal goals and ambitions for the future.

Using the Four Quadrant structure ensures that every area of your life; present and future, has a plan and associated affirmations.

Build On A Strong Foundation

The structure of the Four Quadrants is as important as their content.

Notice that Self and Health form the base level of the framework. These areas are where we need a solid foundation on which we are able to build towards our goals. We can't succeed in life unless we spend time and effort understanding ourselves. Equally without our health, we won't live long enough to achieve or enjoy our aspirations.

Wealth is in the top left corner because, for most of us, having enough money is essential to enable us to reach our goals. It's important to make sure that pursuit of wealth is not a stand-alone goal. You need to understand why you want money (Self) and what you're going to do with it when you get it (Future). Hence Wealth joins the Self and Future Quadrants together.

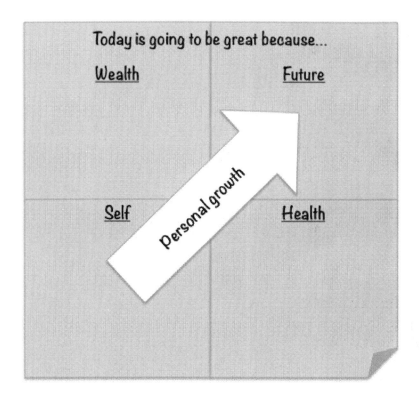

The final Quadrant, Future, is the top of the pile. This is where you ultimately want to end up, personally and professionally. Imagine an arrow like the one in the picture that goes from Self to Future. This is your personal development journey and your path to success!

What Next?

The next step is to fill each Quadrant with affirmations. This humble sheet of paper will then become the roadmap for your life and will help steer you to reaching your ultimate goals.

In the next four chapters, I'm going to talk more about each one of the Quadrants in detail. I'll talk a little bit about what I've learned on the topic from reading and research and then provide some guidance on how to develop your own affirmations for each one.

Self

I said in the previous chapter that Self and Health are the real building blocks of the Four Quadrant framework. If you want to master your goals and achieve success you need to understand who you are and what motivates and drives you. That's what the Self Quadrant is all about.

In this Quadrant, you need to focus on your "Big Why". What are you doing all this for? What really makes you tick? Why do you really want what you want? This is your Big Why and to make the Self Quadrant work you need to find yours. Gary Keller wrote a great book on the importance of prioritizing and focusing on The ONE Thing. Finding your Big Why is all about identifying and focusing on the most important motivation in your life.

The ONE Thing - Gary Keller

Gary Keller is a bestselling real estate author but in this book he focuses on the value of simplifying you workload and focusing on the one most important task in a project. He highlights that multi-tasking isn't the efficiency saving its touted to be and how the concept of work-life balance is more an ideology than a reality. He also explains the concept of time blocking where to allocate set amounts of time to specific individual tasks.

People's Big Whys are very different and often hard to identify. Don't worry if this feels like an impossible task – like finding the meaning of the universe – there is no right answer! I still don't think I truly know my Big Why but I've tried out a lot of medium-sized whys so far and they seem to fit pretty well. Here are a few methods I found useful in approaching this mind-bending challenge.

Five Little Whys leading to One Big Why

The first method I tried to find my Big Why was to adopt a tool made famous by Toyota.

Taiichi Ohno developed the "Five Whys" method to help understand cause and effect relationships in order to resolve a problem.

Basically, you keep asking "Why?" five times until you drive down to the root cause of that issue. I'll give you an example:

My car won't start.
Why?
Because when I turn the key nothing happens.
Why?
Because the battery died.
Why?
Because I left the lights on last night.

Why?
Because I was on the phone when I got out of my car and forgot to turn the lights off.
Why?
Because I had to call my boss and tell him I hadn't done a report that I said I would.

So what we could initially perceive as the problem with the vehicle i.e. the battery is flat; in reality the reason it's flat is my fault. If I had been better organized in planning and managing my day, I would not have been on the phone at the time I pulled into my driveway and would have remembered to shut my lights off.

Not only is the flat battery inconvenient, it's going to cause chaos to the rest of my day. I will now be late, which means I will get further behind with my work and my ability to deliver will get worse and worse. Does this "death spiral" sound familiar in your life? If the slightest thing goes wrong in your day, things seem to escalate quickly until you feel completely overwhelmed, overtired and stressed. That's why taking the time to understand why we are doing things is so important in maintaining positivity and direction when it appears our world is collapsing!

While this example may not have delivered our Big Why, it has just delivered our first potential affirmation for our Self Quadrant:

I will be better organized

Now let's continue our search for our Big Why by digging a bit deeper with the Five Whys. In the flat battery scenario, I have a report with a deadline. How many of us have had a project or task assigned to us with a fixed deadline? On the whole, we are given a reasonable period of time to complete them, but for some reason they just languish in the middle or near the bottom of our to-do list for what appears to be weeks on end. Then all of a sudden, it's the night before the deadline and we instantly have a surge of energy and focus and by some miracle, complete the document on time with minutes to spare.

In this situation, time has come into play and is influencing our Big Why. Our Big Why all along may have been that we want to do a good report to secure a promotion at work but without the time constraint driving us into an inconvenient position; we don't have the necessary levels of motivation to complete the task until the last minute.

Let's go back through the Five Whys principle again with this scenario but expand on the Why questions.

I am rushing to complete a report.
Why?
Because it's due tomorrow.
Why am I doing it now?
Because I want to deliver it on time.
Why does it need to be on time?
Because I want to deliver on my commitment to my manager.
Why do I want to impress my manager?
Because I want a promotion or a bonus.

44

Why do I want more money?
Because I want to pay for my children to go to college.

So by adapting the questions slightly, I've managed to uncover my deep-seated motivation or my Big Why – My Children. They are the reason I get up in the morning, work hard and deliver reports on time so I can provide for them and enable their success.

Try this approach on a few challenges or issues you've had in the last week and see if you get down to one or two common answers at the end. Chances are that on one of these is your Big Why.

Who Are You?

If you don't have success with the Five Whys, another method I've used to find my Big Why is to write out a list of all the roles that I have in my daily life. For now, don't filter them; just write them down as they come to you. Here are some of mine:

I am a son
I am a father
I am an engineer
I am a husband
I am an employee with a solid income
I am a beer drinker
I am a pizza lover

Now take this list and put it in order of which of those roles is the most important to you. Would you rather be an engineer or an employee? Would you rather be a beer drinker than a father? As you go through and compare each of the roles, it soon becomes very obvious which one or two belong at the top of the list. I couldn't decide between these two:

I am a father
I am a husband

At least now I know that either my wife or children or (both!) are my Big Why.

Borrow It!

The two methods I described so far have worked well for me but I appreciate this process isn't easy. Sometimes you may need to shop around before you truly find your Big Why.

There are a number of online sources for inspiration. Just typing "Big Why examples" into Google will give you an endless list of suggestions. Find out more information about people you idolize or want to emulate. Maybe there's friends or people you work who have achieved great success. Why not ask them about their motivation.

Once you've gathered some examples, write down a couple of them and then think back through what you did today.

Did you do anything related to your Big Why today? If so, what was it and how did it make you feel? If it made you happy or grateful or energetic, chances are you're getting close to understanding your Big Why. Perhaps nothing you did today was related to your temporary Big Why. That doesn't mean it's not for you however. How did you feel today overall? If you were sad and frustrated, maybe this could be your Big Why and you're annoyed that you didn't focus on it today.

If you had experiences today that were related to your temporary Big Why but you still felt sad or frustrated, you may need to head back to Google for more inspiration.

Turn Your Big Why into Affirmations

By using one of these methods above you should now have figured out a Big Why – or at least a good temporary one!

The next step is to turn this into some affirmations that you can put into the Self Quadrant. This isn't as daunting as it sounds. Once you understand your motivation, writing down positive statements that nurture and develop it become much easier.

Let's talk through some examples for some popular Big Whys:

If your Big Why is **family,** try:

I will spend more quality time with my family

If it's your **career**, perhaps write:

I will get the promotion I deserve before the end of the year

Or just:

I am great at my job!

Again these are personal statements so yours will be different, but make sure they are positive and related to how you will develop and improve in the area of your life that is most important to you. Refer back to the earlier chapter on Affirmations for more help and guidance.

This is the first Quadrant and these affirmations are focused on you so I can understand they may be hard to write at first.

If you're struggling to get going, you should pick up a copy of You Are A Badass by Jen Sincero. It's brash, motivating and entertaining!

You Are A Badass – Jen Sincero

This is a really entertaining book written by life coach Sincero. She explains how to figure out and fix those behaviors that are in all of us that stop us getting what we want, taking big exciting risks and getting a grip on our personal life. This is an excellent book for helping you figure out who you are and how to make changes so you can kick some ass!

If you still are really stuck, just write down your Big Why for now and you can always come back to it later.

Well done, you're a quarter of the way through building your Four Quadrant life plan! You understand your primary motivation for everything you do and you've got some positive affirmations to reinforce it.

Now you've got your thoughts organized its time to focus on the next important building block to success - your health.

Health

I discussed earlier that without Self and Health there is no point in having any goals or objectives. Our health impacts everything we do. It can enable us if we take care of it or restrict us if we neglect it.

Our health is the most important thing in our lives – without it we're dead! Yet it's the one thing we take for granted most often. It's like our cars. All the time they're running well (healthy) we totally ignore them. We don't' do any proactive maintenance and rarely get the oil changed. But as soon as they break down, our world falls apart. We can't get to work or take the kids to school. We suddenly show it an intense amount of interest and make sure we get the problem fixed.

The way most of us treat our health is the same. We rarely go to the doctor to talk about proactive action we can take. Instead we only go when we're sick. Consequently the discussions and outcomes from the appointment are also more depressing due to all of our "deferred maintenance". At most appointments we get weighed and our blood pressure checked. Invariably both are too high and if your doctor is like mine, they'll also have difficult conversations with you about these while they write the prescription for the actual reason you came in. That puts us off going next time and the spiral continues.

If we all know our health is this important, why don't we take better care of ourselves? Why don't we exercise regularly? Why don't we eat healthily? The answer for me was very simple:

I don't have time.

Finding The Time

Most of us feel we simply don't have the time to take care of ourselves. There are many tasks we have to complete in a day – get up, go to work, eat dinner, pay bills – but going to the gym can always be pushed back to tomorrow...or the day after.

It's either; you don't ever go or you become a gym addict that is always there. We've all seen them in there, high-fiving everyone, drinking protein shakes, always grinning and staring at themselves in the mirror. While we'd like to have their body, everything else about them seems a little bit weird or unstable. You wonder to yourself if they ever go home or what they would do if the gym had to close for a day.

Don't get me wrong, these gym addicts are committed to improving their health, but they never seem well rounded, balanced individuals. Remember that gyms exist for one reason alone, to make money. They rely on people like you and I, signing up for a year, setting up an auto-payment, going for the first few weeks then never coming again. They keep cashing checks without you ever setting foot in the building or using their equipment

To be clear, I'm not anti-gym. Most of them now are becoming more of a community venue and they are a fantastic place to be if you want to push your fitness to the next level. But if you're like me, you want to find a middle ground. A way you can lose weight or reduce your blood pressure without having to spend hundreds of hours or dollars at the gym.

The answer I've found is very simple. Do a little and often. In today's digital world, you don't need a gym membership to do that – or even a fancy DVD box set! Just go to YouTube and search for "7-minute workout", "10-minute workout" or "5-minute abs"; there are absolutely hundreds of free fitness videos out there. Just hit play and start following along.

Everyone can find 5-10 minutes in a day. Stop looking at Facebook or turn off the TV for a few minutes and invest the time in your health. You don't even need to set aside a block of time to do it in. Later I'll give you some suggestions of little ways you can change your daily routine to get more exercise without even thinking!

One of the biggest myths I've encountered with exercise is that you can lose weight by exercising alone. This is nonsense. While exercise helps a little, you need to have the right diet to go with it. If you've ever bought a workout DVD that promises to "transform your body", they all include some kind of meal plan. So from now on when you think about health, think of it as fitness and food. Unfortunately healthy eating is another topic that falls by the wayside in modern chaotic life.

It's Not Just About Fitness

Diet and meals are by far one of the hardest things to control in today's society. We simply don't have the time to spend 2 to 3 hours preparing a glorious, healthy banquet every evening – have you seen how long it takes to cook brown rice!

Consequently, we opt for the quick options and either pick up the phone and use an app or go to the freezer for a frozen pizza. This is where we really need our Health affirmations to kick us into shape!

Like the fitness activities that I described earlier, there are thousands of websites and YouTube videos that will give you guidance on what food to eat and how to create a balanced diet. I'm not going to try and summarize all that material here but what I wanted to share with you some advice or ideas that have worked for me.

Eat Breakfast

Eat breakfast. I have heard breakfast described as the most optimistic meal of the day! If you've been through a solid morning routine, like the Miracle Morning, by the time you get to breakfast you've already got your blood pumping and you're ready to go. Make sure you fuel your body correctly at this pivotal point in your day.

Starting off right with a high protein shake, steel cut oatmeal or fruit and yoghurt can really affect how active and energetic you feel throughout the day. Try and avoid heavy or fried foods like pancakes or sausages as these can weigh you down.

If you have a good healthy breakfast you will be way more optimistic about having other healthy meals during the day.

Be Aware of Calorie Counts

Use calorie information but don't live by it. Calorie counting is a proven way to lose weight, just look at the success of programs like Weight Watchers. The basic principle is obvious, burn more calories than you take on in one day. But the reality of looking up or working out calorie counts for every single meal is cumbersome and depressing.

Doing a little bit of research, you can figure out what the healthier options are – they are normally labeled in grocery stores or highlighted on menus. Some places now even show the calorie values on their menus.

Use all this information as a guide to weigh your various meal choices or ingredients. No need to keep score all day but try and choose a healthier option every day – and don't drown it in a thick creamy dressing!

Snacking is "Death by a Thousand Cuts"

Having cookies left out on the counter or candies in a jar at the office is nothing but an invitation to gain weight. "Out of sight, out of mind" should be your mantra here.

Until you've developed the self-discipline to resist sweet, delicious treats (and when you do, tell me how you did it!) you need to avoid temptation. Again a good solid affirmation here is the key. Easy to say, but you give yourself the best chance of succeeding by hiding those little treats!

No Boozing Has Triple Benefits

I love beer as much as the next person but like smoking cigarettes there is no avoiding the clear health issues that it brings with it. Limiting your intake of alcohol or eliminating it completely can have triple benefits in your life:

- The obvious health benefits associated with not consuming what is basically a toxic substance on a routine basis.
- You substantially reduce your calorie intake. There are a significant amount of calories in beer and even wine. If you're anything like me you've tried light beer and all it means is that you need to drink twice as much. But why not sub in a low carb choice for a few weeks and see how you feel.
- Avoiding alcohol in the evening means you'll sleep better and wake up feeling more refreshed and ready to engage in achieving your goals, rather than feeling slightly fuzzy or poorly rested.

So having a health affirmation around limiting alcohol consumption is a great way to get a big bang for your buck!

Plan Ahead

I've already talked about the importance of having a plan and sticking to it. I realized my inability to plan food and meals was causing my health to deteriorate. So for a number of weeks, I had an affirmation that was simply:

I will plan dinner at breakfast time.

Sometimes this just consisted of looking in the freezer and taking something out to defrost before leaving for work or checking the fridge to make sure I had sufficient vegetables for the meal I planned to cook later that evening. It's the easiest thing in the world to pick up the phone and dial out for pizza or Chinese just because you are one onion short of a decent sauce.

There are an increasing number of companies out there who will deliver all the ingredients and recipe cards for a set of meals right to your door. There are even some that offer healthy eating options. While these may be more expensive than shopping at your local grocery store, they are from my experience, still cheaper than eating out especially as there's no upcharge for drinks.

The great thing about these boxed deliveries is that once you have the menu cards; it gives you some structure and ideas for future dishes that you can buy the ingredients for yourself.

Healthy Affirmations

Hopefully, I've been able to provide you with some inspiration and good ideas for some Health affirmations that you can get excited about! Breaking out of an unhealthy lifestyle is very hard and needs to be taken in baby steps.

Whilst I have made significant strides in achieving a healthy lifestyle I am the first to admit I am nowhere near completion. However understanding the importance of my health to achieving everything else in my life has driven me to give it the necessary focus it deserves.

Please don't think of me as Mr. Scrooge. By all means, go out and invest in gym memberships, exercise equipment and healthy eating recipe books if that works for you. All I was trying to explain in this chapter is that spending money alone cannot take inches off your waist or extend your time on this earth. Motivation and commitment to achieving your affirmations is the only way to do that.

I'm sure your bursting with ideas but here are a few examples of health affirmations that have worked for me are:

I will exercise 5 times a day so I can live to see my kids grow up

I will lose 10lbs by Christmas

Jot down two or three of your own.

Now we've built the Self and Health foundation, its time to talk money!

Wealth

There have been hundreds if not thousands of books written on how to maximize your personal wealth. I've read a few of them but by no means all of them. I should also point out I am not a qualified financial advisor. What I present in this chapter is purely my personal observations from the research I've done and tools that have worked for me.

The summary of my research into how to build your personal wealth essentially boils down to four key themes that seem obvious but most of us just don't do them!

Focus On Things That Bring Money In, Rather Than Take Money Out

Financial education is not sexy or widely publicized. How many of us sit there and watch TV and a commercial comes on with somebody wanting you to buy a rental property or telling you about how to invest for the future? How many of us truly understand what an asset is and what a liability is?

Most of us would think that our home is our greatest asset but when was the last time our home put money in our pocket? Every month, nearly a third of our income goes to pay our mortgage.

Equally, stuff breaks at home that we have to spend lots of money in fixing. Then every now and again, we decide that we want to rip out a perfectly functional bathroom vanity and replace it with a different colored one. No, our home is the greatest drain on our finances.

It's devastating to realize this. Our parents taught us to go out, get a good job, buy a house and settle down. They didn't tell us to go out, get a job, find three more revenue streams and keep improving your financial IQ. I'm not saying we all need to be millionaire real estate investors or successful entrepreneurs, but we all need a level of financial education so we understand what is putting money in our pockets and what is taking it out.

So focus your efforts on finding ways of earning more income rather than spending the money you have. In my opinion (and that of millions of others!) the best book ever written on financial education is Rich Dad Poor Dad by Robert Kiyosaki. His key message is all about understanding your assets and liabilities. Don't go out and buy a new car until you have established a clear source of income to pay for it first.

Rich Dad Poor Dad – Robert Kiyosaki

With tens of millions of copies sold, this book is considered by many as THE book on financial education. Kiyosaki talks about his "two dads," to illustrate some of the common mistakes or misconceptions people have about their personal finances. Poor Dad is his actual father and Rich Dad is the father of his childhood friend. The key messages are the importance of a positive attitude and financial literacy. There are some awesome principles in this book and it's well worth a read!

This was one of the key learning points for me. I made a list of all my assets (what brings money in) and my liabilities (what takes money out). I had one thing in the assets column – my job. Everything else was draining my bank account.

Once you understand this concept, you'll spend your evenings and weekends "shopping" for income sources rather than looking for new, shiny toys! There are some great books out there like "The Four Hour Work Week" by Timothy Ferriss that are bursting with ideas on how to generate extra income – I'll talk more about that book later.

Save More Than You Spend

This is the one that I'd heard time and time again and yet I still find it the hardest to achieve.

When we get a pay rise at work or a refund from our tax return. What's the first thing we do? Spend it on a laptop, dinner or a new stereo. We don't sit there and decide whether to put it in a mutual fund or stocks. No, this is our hard earned money and we deserve a reward.

I have been trying for years to change my mindset on this and I am making progress but it's hard to do in today's consumer society. Before you can start making progress you need to have a compete understanding of your financial picture. When I first did this exercise it was painful and depressing, but understanding where your money is going is vital to improving you financial wellbeing.

It's much easier to do in the digital age and a number of banks and credit card companies provide a great detailed breakdown of your spending. I went online and pulled all my bank statements for the last year and consolidated them all into one spreadsheet. I then sorted them by "Merchant ID" or place I spent the money and categorized every single transaction. Below is a summary of some of the categories I used:

Salary

Merchandise & Supplies

Mortgage

Childcare

Restaurant

Groceries

Utility Bill

Entertainment

Gas

Car Repairs

Car Loan

Insurance

Fees & Adjustments

Babysitting

The results were devastating – I am spending way more than I'm getting!

When I looked back at how much I'd spent on restaurants, takeout, coffee and online shopping; I could have paid for another mortgage. I also could not believe the amount of money that was going out the door every month on credit card interest payments.

There were also hundreds of little charges – for parking or a sandwich – that on their own were insignificant but the volume of them was incredible.

But this data also set me free. I now knew two or three key areas to go and focus on. I made a budget for weekly spending and restaurants, I started taking coffee to work rather than buying it on the way and I printed off a list of all my online shopping items and decided what I didn't need or could return.

Only by understanding these concepts and knowing where all your money is going can you finally start to improve your financial situation. If you can already define a budget and stick to it, great, I applaud you. This Quadrant is going to be enormously easy for you to succeed in.

However if you're anything like me, you'll need to work hard at getting a grip on your financial situation in order to grow your future wealth. You can read all the books you want on how to get rich quick but if you can't account for the pennies you can't account for the millions.

Understand Compound Interest

Once you've figured out how to generate more income and you've stopped spending it all, the next step is to invest it.

We've all heard about the negative side of interest rates (the cost of borrowing money) but very few people understand the power of interest rates when we invest. Compound interest is a miracle of mathematics.

I was one of the fortunate people who enjoyed math in school. Something about numbers and the fact that there was always a right answer really resonated with me. However, at University, I was taught an enormous variety of mathematical techniques: Fourier transforms, differentiation and integration of equations, but I was never taught something as basic as compound interest.

Don't worry if you're not very comfortable with figures, it's a very easy concept and we'll do a little worked example:

From our understanding of our budget, we find **$100** a month that we can invest.

That means we have a total of **$100 x 12 = $1200** to invest in our first year.

We find a high interest savings or investment account that has an interest rate of **5%**.

We check our balance at the end of the first year and we have earned
$1200 x 5% = $60 in interest giving us a total balance of **$1260**.

Our money has grown and we've done nothing but leave it alone!

The best news is it's going to keep growing all the time we leave it there. Take a look at the table below:

YEAR	OPENING BALANCE	PAYMENT	INTEREST RATE	CLOSING BALANCE
1	$ -	$ 1,200	5%	$ 1,260
2	$ 1,260		5%	$ 1,323
3	$ 1,323		5%	$ 1,389
4	$ 1,389		5%	$ 1,459
5	$ 1,459		5%	$ 1,532
TOTAL		$ 1,200		$ 1,532

After 5 years, our lowly **$1200** has grown to **$1532** – that's a **27%** increase for doing nothing!

What if we'd continued to put away that **$100** each month for five years? Our numbers would now look like the table below:

YEAR	OPENING BALANCE	PAYMENT	INTEREST RATE	CLOSING BALANCE
1	$ -	$ 1,200	5%	$ 1,260
2	$ 1,260	$ 1,200	5%	$ 2,583
3	$ 2,583	$ 1,200	5%	$ 3,972
4	$ 3,972	$ 1,200	5%	$ 5,431
5	$ 5,431	$ 1,200	5%	$ 6,962
TOTAL		$ 6,000		$ 6,962

During this 5-year period, we've invested a total of **$6000** that has grown to **$6962**.

See it's that simple! Your money will keep growing and growing provided you put it in stable investments. What should also be abundantly clear is that you don't achieve this stable level or return through lottery tickets or gambling at casinos! This is boring, steady financial growth but this is what all wealthy people do to grow their wealth and the great thing is – you can too!

The Wealthy Barber gives a great explanation of the power of compound interest as well as some great guidance on how to plan for your financial future.

Don't worry it's not as drab as I've just made it sound! It really is a great story.

The Wealthy Barber – David Chilton

This is one of the first financial planning books I ever read and one of the most engaging and understandable. Chilton tells the story of three different people visiting their barber, Roy, on a regular basis and learning a new financial lesson every visit. The key theme of the book is to "save 10 percent of all that you earn and invest it for long-term growth." As well as investing, the book also covers other key personal finance issues like buying a house, tax and life insurance.

There are lots of choices for where to invest your money to take advantage of compound interest. As a general rule, the higher the interest rate (or rate of return) the higher the risk that the investment loses money. While the easiest way to invest may be to just set up a savings account with your bank, these typically have lower interest rates but carry little to no risk. Higher rates can be found with stocks and mutual funds but you'll need to do a little more research before you're able to choose one.

Diversify

One final topic I want to cover is the importance of diversifying your investments. This is just a fancy term for – "don't put all your eggs in one basket"!

We all like to stick with what we know and understand, especially risk adverse engineers like myself. If we work for a shipping company and decide to invest in stocks on the side, chances are we would generally likely to buy stocks in other shipping companies. Equally, if we're in the fortunate position to be awarded stocks in the company we work for, we're likely to hang on to them as a sound investment and a way to share in the profits of the company.

The danger with these strategies is our financial security is directly linked to the success of one company or one particular industry. If there is a decline in your industry and your company is downsizing, you risk losing your job and devaluing all your investments in one go. So you need to make sure you spread your investments around.

Researching other industries or companies can be very time consuming. Fortunately, there are myriad of mutual funds out there that will do this for us.

A mutual fund is basically a professionally managed investment account that pools money from a number of investors like you. The fund manager chooses where to invest the money (stocks and securities) and tries to deliver the best rate of return for the investors. There are also fees associated with these funds that you'll need to understand. An excellent, easy to use tool for getting started with these kinds of funds can be found at www.betterment.com.

Another example of where diversification is important is if you become a property investor. Don't buy all your properties on one street or in one city in case the local economy declines or a natural disaster occurs. Spread your risk exposure across many cities, states or even countries but always be aware of any fees and tax implications.

Set Your Own Goals

For the record, I'll restate that I am not a financial advisor but I have found that all four of the ideas presented here have worked for me. This is the one Quadrant where I'd advise you to do your own specific research or consult a professional.

Once you've done that, it's time to put pen to paper again.

To help you, here's a couple of Wealth affirmations that have worked for me are:

I will cut my monthly spend by $50

I will review all my credit and borrowing and consolidate it

I've found these affirmations to be some of my most dynamic and I'm always tweaking them. Constantly working on improving your finances is a great way to build wealth and ultimately achieve success.

Now all the fundamentals of Self, Health and Wealth are in place it's time to look forward to the Future.

Future

This is by far my favorite Quadrant and the one you can have the most fun with. It's also the one that requires the most soul-searching and, in my experience, the one that changes the most often.

This Quadrant really relies on your understanding of your motivations that you discovered when you wrote your affirmations for the Self Quadrant.

One of the most popular books written on personal development was "The 7 Habits of Highly Effective People" by Stephen Covey.

Seven Habits of Highly Effective People – Stephen R Covey

A fantastic book that focuses on developing your character and ethics. Covey explains that while values govern people's behavior, your character and principles ultimately determine the consequences. He uses the seven habits below to teach how to progress from dependence to independence and ultimate interdependence, where we can be most effective.

1 Be Proactive – don't sit and wait for things to happen
2 Begin with the End in Mind - know where you want to get to before you start
3 Put First Things First - prioritize your activities

---

4 Think Win-Win – find mutually beneficial solutions in all your relationships
5 Seek First to Understand, Then to be Understood – listen to others to truly understand and they will reciprocate
6 Synergize – use teamwork to get outcomes that no individual can achieve
7 Sharpen the Saw – continually seek to improve yourself

I think the second habit really resonates in this Quadrant.

Begin With The End In Mind

While this subheading may sound morbid when you first hear it, understand that it doesn't mean the end of your life; here "the end" means your ultimate goal or your "end game". In order to develop affirmations around it for this Quadrant, you have to have a pretty good idea of what it is.

How to best approach and understand your "end game" depends on the way your mind works. Being an engineer I lean towards lists, numbers and metrics to establish a goal rather than visual images. However, I appreciate the value in both approaches so here are two methods I've used to try and understand where I ultimately want to end up.

Let's start with the engineering approach!

Your Perfect Day

The first step in this approach is to write down your ideal day.

Start off with when and where do you want to wake up? What do you want to do as soon as you get up? (Hopefully it's exercise and Four Quadrant affirmations!) After breakfast, do you head out of the door to work? Do you want to take your children to school? Do you want to jump in your truck and drive to a construction site? Do you want to sit on the couch and play video games or go and have a round of golf?

Remember to keep it somewhat realistic – no playing table tennis on the moon for example. Similarly you won't be doing the same thing every day but try and get down the important elements.

Where would you like to eat lunch and who would you like to eat lunch with? Then after lunch what next? Some meetings? Who with? On the golf course? With your business partner? Discussing your latest technology venture? Maybe you want to take a walk on the beach? Or sit by a fire with a good book?

Finally let's look at the evening. How would you like to spend that? At the movie theater? Sampling street cuisine on the streets of Bangkok? Where do you want to go to bed? Who do you want to say goodnight to?

If you're stuck for ideas, a fantastic book to get some inspiration for your perfect day is "The 4-Hour Workweek" by Timothy Ferriss.

The 4-Hour Workweek - Timothy Ferriss

A really motivational book that inspired me to write mine! Ferriss' key message is that truly wealthy people (the "New Rich") don't necessarily have millions in the bank; they have time and freedom too so they can truly live and enjoy their life. This book gives lots of practical, honest advice on how to achieve your perfect lifestyle.

The key themes are summarized by Ferriss' acronym "DEAL" which stands for:

Definition: Really understand what you're trying to do and get rid of all negative assumptions.
Elimination: Ignore the less important stuff to give yourself more *time*.
Automation: Automate your *income* generating activities.
Liberation: Get the *mobility* to work from anywhere.

Next, look at what you've just written and try and understand the key things you need to have in place to achieve those activities. Start writing down some of these key "enablers" of your perfect day.

Be careful not to just say "I need to be rich"! When you really focus on what you want, you may not need to be a millionaire. Is an abundance of money really necessary if your idea of happiness is camping on the beach? Having lots of cash is not necessarily essential to achieving the life of your dreams. Most of us spend a third of our monthly income on a mortgage payment. If our mortgage was paid off we may not be cash rich but we would be wealthy.

Try and think beyond money and look at how your life would need to be set up. If you want to spend all day on the golf course you may need to have a partner or childcare that would enable you to do that. Equally, if you want to meet with your business partner, you need to have a business to discuss with them!

Once you've got 4 or 5 key criteria or enablers for achieving your perfect day, it's now time to think of affirmations that would help you achieve those enablers. For example:

If your perfect day has you playing golf, try:

I will learn to play golf

Or if you don't want to work so you can take your children to school, how about:

I will have a financial structure in place to enable me to live without having to work

Keep a copy of your perfect day so you can refer back to it in the future and tick items off as you make progress. I keep mine taped inside the closet door so I see it every morning when I go to get dressed.

If that approach didn't work for you or you struggled to visualize what your perfect day would look like, let's try something a little more hands-on!

Your Dream Board

We all have dreams. They start at a very young age:

I want to be a racecar driver

As we get older, we become more cynical and jaded and we lose sight of our dreams or become embarrassed by them. We lose the ability to think creatively about the future.

77

You're currently a level one manager in a large corporation. What's your dream job? To become a level two manager? How dull. I'm sure the seven-year-old version of you would roll their eyes and walk out the room at this point. But we've become so entrenched in what we are doing day-to-day, we lose the ability to look up over the parapet and understand where we would really like to be. What we would like to be doing and how we would really like to be living.

That's where the dream board comes in!

A dream board is a visual way of capturing your dreams and ambitions. As with previous topics, there's a wealth of information on this topic and some great inspiration on sites like Pintrest. I'm just going to summarize here how I created mine.

1. **Grab loads of magazines – digitally or paper.**

   Try and find magazines with a lot of glossy pictures in. Try to avoid magazines that you may read regularly in order to get you thinking outside of your comfort zone.

   Flick through those magazines and look for pictures that resonate with you. Don't over think it at this point, if you see something shiny put a ring around it with a Sharpie or cut it out immediately with a pair of scissors. Work through as many magazines as you can until you've got a good collection of images on the floor.

For those of you who are doing this digitally, download your files to one folder. I found it easier to print them all together at the end of this step. However if you are a whizz with Photoshop, you can keep it all in digital format for now.

While you are gathering images, also try looking for words or phrases that stimulate you or maybe go online and a find list of famous quotes.

2. **Arrange your images together in groups**

Once you've got a good stack of material, start arranging the images into groups. I find this helps my mind absorb them. You can even use the Four Quadrant headings here to help you.

Group together those that are related to your development and your family in Self or Future.

Put those related to money or fitness in the Wealth and Health piles.

Once you're happy with your groups, find a big piece of card and stick them to it.

For those who are more computer savvy, arrange them on the screen in groups and print the whole board off in color.

3. **Put it somewhere visible.**

It helps to look at your dream board every day so you keep the images in your mind as you go through the day. This is something I initially struggled with as I didn't want every visitor to my house to have a window into my soul and see my ambitions. But you'd be amazed how many people don't notice it or don't even make a passing comment on it. At the end of the day, this is about you and your dreams, not about what other people think.

Similar to your Perfect Day, now you need to stare at your Dream Board and start thinking about those things you need to do to enable this lifestyle. Again try and write down 4 or 5 sentences that you can use as the basis of your Future affirmations.

What To Do Next

Now you understand where you want to go, write down two or three affirmations that will get you there.

You've probably already got some from your list of enablers but if not, here are two Future affirmations that have worked for me:

I will live on a lake

I will create and grow my own business

Congratulations, now all the Four Quadrants are complete! Hopefully your staring at a sheet of paper covered in some inspiring, harmonized statements that clearly show the direction you want your life to go.

There's one last thing you need to do that is essential to getting you going in the direction you've now so clearly defined - take action.

Take Action

Now comes the bit that 95% of people never do - take action.

There is a widely used Wayne Gretzky quote I want to insert here:

You miss 100 percent of the shots you never take.

This is perfect context for what we're going to cover in this chapter. If you never take any action, you will never achieve your goals.

You can have the best, most eloquent affirmations ever written in your Four Quadrants, but unless you actually do something to achieve them, this whole exercise has been wasted energy.

Take Baby Steps

Taking action is by far the hardest part of any new activity but it's much easier if you take small steps first.

How often have you started a new fitness regime only to fail within the first few days? You've decided you want to run a marathon. You go out to buy a new set of specialist running shoes, you pour over running websites and buy yourself a tracking GPS watch. You sign up for either a gym or a running club.

The first day you put on your brand new gear, stretch all your muscles properly and set off to run. You can just run and run and run. It feels like you can run a marathon on the first day and you cover more miles in that one session that you have done all year. Wow, this is easy! You give yourself a big pat on the back and that night you celebrate with a beer and a burger.

The next day, you get up and you're so stiff you can barely move. You give yourself a pass today as you did such an awesome job yesterday. Day three rolls in and you're still hurting. You move your running shoes into the closet so you don't trip over them. Day four, you have to work late so you miss your running time.

Days turn into weeks and slowly but surely you forget all about your training. Your fancy running shoes migrate to the back of the closet - never to be seen again. Maybe one of your friends will ask you a week or so later; "How's your new running regime going?" "Oh, I didn't take to it" will be your reply.

Why did you fail?

You may have heard phrases like, "you can't swallow an elephant" or "don't try and boil the ocean!" When I've looked back at my previous failures, both personally and professionally, I have always tried to do too much, too soon.

Our modern society encourages us to "think big" or "dream big". While enormous goals are great for motivating people, you still need to *do* something to achieve them. I've found that small, precise actions that are measurable and achievable are the best way to get things done.

For example, when I wrote this book, rather than sitting down to write it in one go, I broke it down into topics and chapters. I then researched each individual topic and starting building the book chapter by chapter. By breaking up the task it became more manageable. I could also see myself making progress as I completed each chapter, which was a great motivation to keep going.

The same is true for actions you need to take to achieve your affirmations. You need to break them out into smaller pieces that you can stack together to reach your ultimate goal.

In The 7 Habits, Covey emphasizes the importance of putting first things first. That mantra is a great one to bear in mind while identifying actions for each affirmation. If your affirmation is to own a lake house, don't make your first action to drive around all the lakes in your local area looking for properties. You need to focus on your finances first and understand your affordability before you can start shopping.

Write Down Your Actions Daily

Now let's take this concept of small actions and apply it to our Four Quadrant affirmations.

Take your sheet of Four Quadrants and at the bottom of each sections write:

"...and I will take one action today to achieve this."

That simple sentence is how you're going to drive each one of your affirmations to become a reality and allow you to achieve success.

For this next part, you're going to need a notebook. This is the one thing I would say is worth investing a little bit of money in. It doesn't have to be fancy or leather bound with the expensive paper, but it does need to be sturdy as you are going to carry it with you on a daily basis. I found a nice Moleskin one that has a bookmarker and a pocket inside the back cover. This is a great place to keep your Four Quadrant sheet. You'll need a pen or pencil too!

Every day for each one of the Four Quadrants, you'll be writing down one action that you're going to take to make the affirmations in that Quadrant become reality.

Remember the key is to start small to achieve big. Let's take an example from the Wealth Quadrant.

Say you write an affirmation in the Wealth Quadrant like this:

I will reduce my monthly spend by $50 a month.

You know from the budgeting activity you did to develop this affirmation that you spend $20 a month on coffee. So just write down a simple action that says:

I won't buy a coffee today.

Look, now you've just saved yourself $3-4, so only $46 more to find this month! I try and build on my actions each day, so the next day don't buy a coffee and write another action that says:

I will bring in leftovers for lunch

Now in two days, you've saved on two coffees ($8) and one sandwich ($7) so you only need to find $35 more savings this month.

Another good example is an action I have used for the Health Quadrant:

I will park my car in the furthest spot from the entrance

This is so easy to do and it means you get that little bit of extra exercise without having to get your running shoes on!

I started this action one summer in the parking lot at my office. It was so easy to begin with and I felt great - strolling in the sunshine! When winter came, it was much more tempting to park nearer to door but I actually found the cold, wind and rain invigorating and a great way to help me get energized for the day!

Get Creative

You need to write new actions every day so be creative with them. I relish the challenge of trying to find new and exciting ways to inch closer to my affirmations. Here's one of my personal favorites that I dreamt up for the Wealth Quadrant. Against my affirmation of

I will reduce my monthly spend by $50 a month.

I wrote:

I will cut my toenails.

By now you probably think I've gone crazy but hear me out. The day before, I ripped a massive hole in one of my socks because my little toenail had grown into a sharp point. This had cost me $6 for a new pair of socks.

By taking the simple action of cutting my toenail today I will save myself another $6 pair of socks so I am getting closer to my goal. Don't forget this is all about controlling your outgoings and avoiding unnecessary extra costs.

This is a shining example of how having the Four Quadrant structure and very specific actions can make even the most mundane of personal grooming chores feel like progress towards improving your life.

Have Some Fall-Back Options

While I enjoy the challenge of developing a new action every day, we can't always be that creative. In these situations one of the most powerful techniques I found is to simply write:

I won't walk past a problem.

While this may not sound dynamic, it is something that will keep me actively looking for problems in my life throughout the day and take action to fix them.

Let's take an example. You have an affirmation that says:

I will support my partner in their new business endeavor.

While in the early days of focusing on this affirmation it was easy to dream up new actions like taking the children to school so she could make an early meeting or cooking dinner so she could talk to her client, after a few weeks I was running low on fresh ideas.

This is where I first used the "don't walk past a problem" action. It made me do simple things like picking up the laundry off the floor and putting it in the washing machine. That small act took a minute at best but it can make a significant difference to our lives together.

If she had come home from a hard day trying to build a new business and the bedroom was covered in my dirty underwear and T-shirts, chances are the situation was going to escalate. Finishing an already stressful day by having an argument would mean she wouldn't sleep well or start her next day off right. Creating this negative situation isn't being very supportive of her new business endeavor.

I'm not saying that we all need to become house cleaners in order to best support our partners but taking one or two minutes a day to do a considerate thing, no matter how little, helps. My action here actually contributed to our joint happiness and overall success.

Keep Score

The great thing about writing down these actions every day is we have a record to refer to.

I keep my notebook with me throughout the day and as I achieve each action I cross it off the list. Remember earlier when I talked about the importance of tracking progress? This is a great way to do that in a very measurable way.

Each day you can give yourself a score and see a tangible measure of your progress. Don't worry if you don't achieve all your actions. This is a marathon, not a sprint. The main thing is you are taking steps towards realizing your affirmations every day. You have direction and you are marching towards success. You also have written proof, in your own handwriting that you're getting there.

Some days I only manage to achieve one or two actions. That's fine! I'm still two steps closer to achieving my ultimate goals than I was yesterday. Some days I decide to roll over actions from one day to the next due to circumstances beyond my control like the pool I was going to take my children swimming in was closed unexpectedly.

However like cellphone contracts, there needs to be a finite number of times you roll over an action. One or two days should be the absolute maximum. If you haven't done it by then it's either not important or you're not fully committed to achieving the affirmation it's linked to.

Get Doing!

I can't overstate the importance of taking action in order to achieve success in your life.

You will eternally be a "victim" of bad luck or unfortunate events until you step up and start taking action to improve your life.

The next chapter lays out a clear plan to getting your Four Quadrants working for you. All you need to do is take action and follow it!

Your First Week

You've now got all the tools you need to truly unscramble your life, regain your direction and achieve success. All you need to do is start using them!

The Four Quadrant method relies on your commitment to establishing a series of habits and routines in order to make yourself successful.

This chapter lays out how to start forming these new routines in just a week. It builds on what Hal Elrod describes in his Miracle Morning book.

It will help you build your Four Quadrant framework and start getting you into some great habits. In just seven days you'll start to feel more in control of your life, more energetic and more focused on your future.

Let's start today!

DAY 1

Time to do a little bit of prep work, there are five things you need to do to get ready.

1. Lay out your workout clothes.

The last thing you want to be doing on the first day of your new lifestyle is fumbling around in the dark trying to find some clothes to put on.

Nothing will kill your positivity faster than getting increasingly frustrated as you rummage through the very back of your drawer to find that elusive pair of shorts.

2. Get your tools ready.

This sounds more complicated than it is. Find a notepad and a pen. Put them somewhere obvious for the morning. You'll also need your Perfect Day or Dream board handy.

3. Identify a space

Find somewhere in your home where you can have some time alone in the early hours of the morning.

4. Set an alarm

I talked a lot about the importance of getting out of bed early and this is the absolute key to starting off your first week.

Set your alarm clock for an hour earlier than you would normally get up. Put it across the room if you're nervous about using the snooze button!

5. Before you fall asleep, recite one affirmation.

Work out how many hours sleep you will get between now and your horrendously early alarm clock time. Maybe it's six hours. Immediately before you fall asleep tell yourself:

"Six hours is plenty of sleep and I'm going to feel refreshed in the morning."

Sweet dreams – tomorrow is going to be awesome!

DAY 2

Okay, this is where the rubber meets the road.

Get out of bed – well done! Now let's get the blood flowing with a little bit of exercise.

The key here is not to overdo it. If you like running and have good shoes, go for a little run – only 10 to 15 minutes. If you don't like running, go to YouTube and find a 7-10 minute workout video for beginners and follow it.

Feels good, doesn't it? Now you've got your heart rate up it's time to exercise your mind. Grab a piece of paper, fold it in four, put down the Four Quadrant headings and start writing affirmations!

As I've said a few times, they don't need to be perfect but try and get something in each box. Don't forget to write "Today is going to be great because..." on the top of the page.

Your final task for today is to stand up straight, push your shoulders back and take a deep breath.

Hold your Four Quadrants out in front of you and recite them one after the other going from Self to Health to Wealth then Future.

Finish with a "Today is going to be great because..." statement.

Feel the power and positive energy flowing through you? Don't worry if you don't, it will come!

Now it's time to go and start another great day!

DAY 3

I didn't say it yesterday but Day 2 and 3 are the hardest ones to get out of bed for. Your body is in shock on Day 1 but by now it's starting to know what you're up to!

Congratulate yourself on sticking with the program and don't worry, it does get easier!

Today is a great day to adopt the Miracle Morning SAVERS routine. Here's a quick reminder of what it is:

The Miracle Morning "SAVERS" acronym- Hal Elrod

Silence – first take time to meditate and relax
Affirmations – focus on your goals
Visualizations – visualize your goals
Exercise – get your blood pumping
Reading – educate yourself
Scribing – take notes or journal

Start by sitting in silence for a few minutes. Try and clear your mind of all thoughts.

Next grab your Four Quadrant piece of paper with your awesome affirmations from yesterday on. For the second "SAVERS" step, just start reciting them.

Are they starting to feel more normal?

Why not use your Visualization time to imagine yourself living your perfect day from the Future Quadrant?

Use the Reading time to refresh yourself on the Take Actions chapter because that's just what we're going to do in the Scribing slot!

Write down at least one action per Quadrant – if you can manage one per affirmation that would be excellent. Remember to make them simple and achievable because you're going to do them all today!

That's right; take your notebook with you and throughout Day 3 check off the actions as you achieve them. I try and do as many as possible at the end of my morning routine before I begin the workday and other distractions creep in!

DAY 4

We're going to add two more things today.

First of all, we've got to find a new book! Much as I'd love you to read my book every day, it's going to get pretty stale and boring after a while, so go out and find some new material to inspire and develop you

Use your Reading time today to research and buy what you're going to read next.

Perhaps you want to read one of the books I've referenced in earlier chapters or maybe you have a specific subject you want to understand in more detail – like retirement planning or dealing stocks.

Amazon is a great place to find reading material on thousands of subjects and with e-books, that material can be in your hands in seconds. If you need more inspiration, my website has a list of some of the most recent books I've read: **www.unscrambleyourlife.com**

Your second task today is to review your actions from yesterday and score yourself. How many did you complete? 50%? 80%? 100%? If you got a really low score try and understand why. Were your actions too difficult to fit into one day? If so, try and simplify them into more bite-size chunks.

If you didn't get to them all, replay the day in your head and find a time where you could have done them but you decided to watch TV instead or check Facebook.

The speed at which you can get your life on track and reach the levels of success you want is directly linked to your ability to complete these actions. If you're truly serious about realizing your affirmations then you need to identify those distractions that are wasting your time and stop them.

Now make one of your actions today to write down those things that are stopping you from progressing on your goals and start identifying ways to get rid of them.

DAY 5

It is time to start your new book today!

Carve out 15-20 minutes to really get stuck into it. During your Scribing time, jot down a few notes on what you've read today. Making written notes helps your brain learn and absorb new concepts.
My notebook is packed full of summaries of books I've read. I just write down one to two bullet points per chapter to help me remember some of the concepts presented. It helps stimulate my memory when I need to refer back to them later.

DAY 6

Now it's time to look back at your affirmations and tweak them.

You've been saying them for four days now so you must have identified some improvements you can make. You have to respect and truly believe in your affirmations so you can't afford for them to be substandard.

As well as word-smithing, take a step back and make sure you haven't missed anything. Think about your Big Why - do all your affirmations fully align with it? If not, edit, delete or add to them.

DAY 7

Congratulations you've made it through your first week!

You've gone from drifting through life in a chaotic way to establishing a direction and taking steps to achieving your ultimate goals. You should feel good about yourself.

If you haven't already, tell others about your week. Tell them about my book (shameless plug!) or the book you've started reading. Remember Covey's Seven Habits is all about striving towards interdependence so listening to others and building on their feedback and ideas is a great way to increase your personal effectiveness.

After you've given yourself a pat on the back, it's time for one last task today – pay it forward.

I've talked a lot about the power of positive energy and what better way to build it than by helping others. Pay for someone's coffee in the drive-thru line, bring donuts into work, cook dinner for your family or donate to charity. Just give - no matter how small and feel the positive energy flow.

Beyond Seven Days

What do you do on Day 8? Don't panic! Remember that you're trying to form new habits and break down some old ones.

There's lots of material out there that will help you do this but one that I found particularly useful is "The Power of Habit" by Charles Duhigg.

The Power of Habit - Charles Duhigg

Pulitzer-prize winning author Duhigg has written the definitive book on habits. From years of in depth research he's identified the 3-step loop that drives our habits:
Cue - the trigger that initiates the behavior.
Routine - the behavior itself or the action you take.
Reward - the benefit you gain from doing the behavior.
You can successfully alter or adopt new habits by changing just the routine part. Finally Duhigg outlines the three ways to grow your willpower:

1. Do something that requires a lot of discipline – like your Miracle Morning!

2. Plan ahead for worst-case scenarios – anticipate bad news and be ready to respond positively

3. Preserve your autonomy – our willpower is at its lowest with must-do tasks assigned to us by others. Own your life and control the tasks you do to succeed.

Let's look at how Duhigg's research can help us establish our Four Quadrants as part of our daily lives.

Firstly, place your Four Quadrants somewhere visible. Stuck on the bathroom mirror or bedside table or in the kitchen by the coffee pot. By displaying them clearly, they remind us of the commitment we have made to improve our lifestyle. Seeing these affirmations triggers (or *cues*) us to start our *routine*.

After we've recited our affirmations and decided why today is going to be great, we record all the actions we are going to take today to achieve those goals.

Finally, we review yesterday's actions and check them off. By completing actions, we can see demonstrated progress towards achieving our lifestyle goals and feel good about ourselves for the progress we're making.

This positive feeling is our *reward*. We are also getting the longer-term rewards of good health, financial freedom and are getting closer to our ultimate dream lifestyle.

Positivity is what motivates us to start the loop all over again tomorrow and the next day. Keep driving for those positive feelings and the good habits will come!

Over To You

As I said at the beginning, I am sharing the Four Quadrant concept and other tools with you to help you achieve what I did - an unscrambled life.

They are my gift to you - please take them and make them your own.

I would love to hear about how you are using and adapting them to find direction and success in your life.

Please get in touch via my website (**www.unscrambleyourlife.com**) or write me a review on Amazon.

My website also contains my latest book reviews as well as my blog and some further sources of inspiration and motivation.

Thank you for taking the time to read my book.

I wish you every success.

About Nick Salmon

Nick is a son, husband, father, engineer, employee, beer drinker and pizza lover.

He is thirtysomething and lives in the USA with his wife and two children.

Nick is happier and more productive today than he has ever been thanks to the concepts outlined in this book.

He is excited to share them with you.

Made in the USA
San Bernardino, CA
05 November 2018